pause & reflect

MEDITATIONS FOR JUSTICE

T0163696

pause & reflect

MEDITATIONS FOR JUSTICE

ONE VOICE PRESS

WILMETTE, ILLINOIS

One Voice Press
401 Greenleaf Avenue, Wilmette, Illinois
60091

Printed in the United States of America on
acid-free paper ∞

ISBN: 978-1-61851-182-9
23 22 21 20   4 3 2 1

Cover design by Carlos Esparza
Book design by Patrick Falso

CONTENTS

Introduction... 1

Justice.. 5

Courage 63

Action 87

INTRODUCTION

"The best beloved of all things in My sight is Justice," states Bahá'u'lláh in the Hidden Words, "turn not away therefrom if thou desirest Me, and neglect it not that I may confide in thee. By its aid thou shalt see with thine own eyes and not through the eyes of others, and shalt know of thine own knowledge and not through the knowledge of thy neighbor. Ponder this in thy heart; how it behooveth thee to be. Verily justice is My gift to thee and the sign of My loving-kindness. Set it then before thine eyes."*

This third title in the *Pause & Reflect* series was put together with a certain degree of urgency. Its theme, justice, is a subject surely at the forefront of the minds of many people throughout the world at the present time. *Pause*

---

* Bahá'u'lláh, the Hidden Words, Arabic, no. 2.

& Reflect is a series that presents meditative passages from the writings of the Bahá'í Faith arranged around particular themes. While the Bahá'í Faith places a great deal of importance on meditation and the cultivation of spirituality, it is also a religion that calls for action and societal transformation. Meditation, from a Bahá'í perspective, is not exclusively a means for personal growth but also a tool that should equip us with insights and awareness that can be translated into action in our lives and in the communities in which we live.

Far from being purely the domain of institutions and courts, justice is a principle worthy of our deepest reflection. In the words of 'Abdu'l-Bahá: "Justice is not limited, it is a universal quality. Its operation must be carried out in all classes, from the highest to the lowest. Justice must be sacred, and the rights of all the people must be considered. Desire for others only that which you desire for yourselves. Then shall we rejoice in the Sun of Justice, which shines from the Horizon of God."*

Everywhere we look, symptoms of societal ills—such as systemic racism, the oppression of people of color, gender inequality, the

---

* 'Abdu'l-Bahá, *Paris Talks,* no. 49.15–16.

extremes of wealth and poverty—are glaringly apparent, and threaten the well-being of people and communities throughout the world. At the core of the message of the Bahá'í Faith is the oneness of humankind and the equality of all peoples. Many of the quotations presented here place justice within the context of race and prejudice. This is not accidental. The unity in diversity that the Faith calls for, and for which its community strives, cannot be achieved without justice. This small book is not intended as a comprehensive volume on the subject but merely offers a selection of short extracts that invite meditation and reflection. It is hoped that readers will find the time and space to ponder the passages deeply, to draw insight from them, and to seek ways to apply that insight to their lives and communities.

Justice

BAHÁ'U'LLÁH

1

There is no force on earth that can equal in its conquering power the force of justice and wisdom. I, verily, affirm that there is not, and hath never been, a host more mighty than that of justice and wisdom. . . . There can be no doubt whatever that if the daystar of justice, which the clouds of tyranny have obscured, were to shed its light upon men, the face of the earth would be completely transformed.

2

I beseech Thee, O my God, by all the transcendent glory of Thy Name, to clothe Thy loved ones in the robe of justice and to illumine their beings with the light of trustworthiness. Thou art the One that hath power to do as He pleaseth and Who holdeth within His grasp the reins of all things, visible and invisible.

3

We entreat God to deliver the light of equity and the sun of justice from the thick clouds of waywardness, and cause them to shine forth upon men. No light can compare with the light of justice. The establishment of order in the world and the tranquility of the nations depend upon it.

4

By the righteousness of God! Justice is a powerful force. It is, above all else, the conqueror of the citadels of the hearts and souls of men, and the revealer of the secrets of the world of being, and the standard-bearer of love and bounty.

5

The light of men is Justice. Quench it not with the contrary winds of oppression and tyranny. The purpose of justice is the appearance of unity among men. The ocean of divine wisdom surgeth within this exalted word, while the books of the world cannot contain its inner significance. Were mankind to be adorned with this raiment, they would behold the daystar of the utterance, "On that day God will satisfy everyone out of His abundance,"* shining resplendent above the horizon of the world.

---

* Qur'án 4:129.

6

Say: "O God, my God! Attire mine head with the crown of justice, and my temple with the ornament of equity. Thou, verily, art the Possessor of all gifts and bounties."

Justice and equity are twin Guardians that watch over men. From them are revealed such blessed and perspicuous words as are the cause of the well-being of the world and the protection of the nations.

7

O Son of Spirit! The best beloved of all things in My sight is Justice; turn not away therefrom if thou desirest Me, and neglect it not that I may confide in thee. By its aid thou shalt see with thine own eyes and not through the eyes of others, and shalt know of thine own knowledge and not through the knowledge of thy neighbor. Ponder this in thy heart; how it behooveth thee to be. Verily justice is My gift to thee and the sign of My loving-kindness. Set it then before thine eyes.

8

They that are just and fair-minded in their judgement occupy a sublime station and hold an exalted rank. The light of piety and uprightness shineth resplendent from these souls. We earnestly hope that the peoples and countries of the world may not be deprived of the splendors of these two luminaries.

9

Unto the emblems of justice and the exponents of equity it is indubitably clear and evident that this Wronged One, strengthened by the transcendent power of the Kingdom, is seeking to efface from among the peoples and kindreds of the earth every evidence of disorder, discord, dissension, differences or divisions; and it is for no other reason but this great, this momentous object that He hath again and again been cast into prison and many a day and a night hath been subjected to chains and fetters.

10

Justice is, in this day, bewailing its plight, and Equity groaneth beneath the yoke of oppression. The thick clouds of tyranny have darkened the face of the earth, and enveloped its peoples.

11

Be vigilant, that ye may not do injustice to anyone, be it to the extent of a grain of mustard seed. Tread ye the path of justice, for this, verily, is the straight path.

12

Exert yourselves that ye may attain this transcendent and most sublime station, the station that can ensure the protection and security of all mankind. This goal excelleth every other goal, and this aspiration is the monarch of all aspirations. So long, however, as the thick clouds of oppression, which obscure the daystar of justice, remain undispelled, it would be difficult for the glory of this station to be unveiled to men's eyes.

13

Say: No man can attain his true station except through his justice. No power can exist except through unity. No welfare and no well-being can be attained except through consultation.

14

He Who is your Lord, the All-Merciful, cherisheth in His heart the desire of beholding the entire human race as one soul and one body. Haste ye to win your share of God's good grace and mercy in this Day that eclipseth all other created Days. How great the felicity that awaiteth the man that forsaketh all he hath in a desire to obtain the things of God! Such a man, We testify, is among God's blessed ones.

'ABDU'L-BAHÁ

15

The second attribute of perfection is justice and impartiality. This means to have no regard for one's own personal benefits and selfish advantages, and to carry out the laws of God without the slightest concern for anything else. It means to see one's self as only one of the servants of God, the All-Possessing, and except for aspiring to spiritual distinction, never attempting to be singled out from the others. It means to consider the welfare of the community as one's own. It means, in brief, to regard humanity as a single individual, and one's own self as a member of that corporeal form, and to know of a certainty that if pain or injury afflicts any member of that body, it must inevitably result in suffering for all the rest.

16

And the breeding-ground of all these tragedies is prejudice: prejudice of race and nation, of religion, of political opinion; and the root cause of prejudice is blind imitation of the past—imitation in religion, in racial attitudes, in national bias, in politics. So long as this aping of the past persisteth, just so long will the foundations of the social order be blown to the four winds, just so long will humanity be continually exposed to direst peril.

17

And the honor and distinction of the individual consist in this, that he among all the world's multitudes should become a source of social good. Is any larger bounty conceivable than this, that an individual, looking within himself, should find that by the confirming grace of God he has become the cause of peace and well-being, of happiness and advantage to his fellow men? No, by the one true God, there is no greater bliss, no more complete delight.

18

... acts of cooperation, mutual assistance and reciprocity are not confined to the body and to things that pertain to the material world, but for all conditions, whether physical or spiritual, such as those related to minds, thoughts, opinions, manners, customs, attitudes, understandings, feelings or other human susceptibilities. In all these thou shouldst find these binding relationships securely established. The more this interrelationship is strengthened and expanded, the more will human society advance in progress and prosperity. Indeed without these vital ties it would be wholly impossible for the world of humanity to attain true felicity and success.

19

Justice is not limited, it is a universal quality. Its operation must be carried out in all classes, from the highest to the lowest. Justice must be sacred, and the rights of all the people must be considered.

Every human being has the right to live; they have a right to rest, and to a certain amount of well-being. As a rich man is able to live in his palace surrounded by luxury and the greatest comfort, so should a poor man be able to have the necessaries of life. Nobody should die of hunger; everybody should have sufficient clothing; one man should not live in excess while another has no possible means of existence.

Let us try with all the strength we have to bring about happier conditions, so that no single soul may be destitute.

20

We ask God to endow human souls with justice so that they may be fair, and may strive to provide for the comfort of all, that each member of humanity may pass his life in the utmost comfort and welfare. Then this material world will become the very paradise of the Kingdom, this elemental earth will be in a heavenly state and all the servants of God will live in the utmost joy, happiness and gladness. We must all strive and concentrate all our thoughts in order that such happiness may accrue to the world of humanity.

21

I hope that each one of you will become just, and direct your thoughts towards the unity of mankind; that you will never harm your neighbors nor speak ill of any one; that you will respect the rights of all men, and be more concerned for the interests of others than for your own. Thus will you become torches of Divine justice, acting in accordance with the Teaching of Bahá'u'lláh, who, during His life, bore innumerable trials and persecutions in order to show forth to the world of mankind the virtues of the World of Divinity, making it possible for you to realize the supremacy of the spirit, and to rejoice in the Justice of God.

22

Desire for others only that which you desire for yourselves. Then shall we rejoice in the Sun of Justice, which shines from the Horizon of God.

23

Among the results of the manifestation of spiritual forces will be that the human world will adapt itself to a new social form, the justice of God will become manifest throughout human affairs, and human equality will be universally established.

24

I shall ask you a question: Did God create us for love or for enmity? Did He create us for peace or discord? Surely He has created us for love; therefore, we should live in accordance with His will. Do not listen to anything that is prejudiced, for self-interest prompts men to be prejudiced. They are thoughtful only of their own will and purposes. They live and move in darkness.

25

. . . Bahá'u'lláh set forth principles of guidance and teaching for economic readjustment. Regulations were revealed by Him which ensure the welfare of the commonwealth. As the rich man enjoys his life surrounded by ease and luxuries, so the poor man must, likewise, have a home and be provided with sustenance and comforts commensurate with his needs. This readjustment of the social economy is of the greatest importance inasmuch as it ensures the stability of the world of humanity; and until it is effected, happiness and prosperity are impossible.

26

Strive, therefore, to create love in the hearts in order that they may become glowing and radiant. When that love is shining, it will permeate other hearts even as this electric light illumines its surroundings. When the love of God is established, everything else will be realized. This is the true foundation of all economics. Reflect upon it. Endeavor to become the cause of the attraction of souls rather than to enforce minds. Manifest true economics to the people. Show what love is, what kindness is, what true severance is and generosity. This is the important thing for you to do. Act in accordance with the teachings of Bahá'u'lláh. All His Books will be translated. Now is the time for you to live in accordance with His words. Let your deeds be the real translation of their meaning. Economic questions will not attract hearts. The love of God alone will attract them. Economic questions are most interesting; but the power which moves, controls and attracts the hearts of men is the love of God.

27

. . . Bahá'u'lláh taught that an equal standard of human rights must be recognized and adopted. In the estimation of God all men are equal; there is no distinction or preferment for any soul in the dominion of His justice and equity.

28

Concerning the prejudice of race: it is an illusion, a superstition pure and simple! For God created us all of one race. There were no differences in the beginning, for we are all descendants of Adam. In the beginning, also, there were no limits and boundaries between the different lands; no part of the earth belonged more to one people than to another. In the sight of God there is no difference between the various races. Why should man invent such a prejudice? . . .

God has not created men that they should destroy one another. All races, tribes, sects and classes share equally in the Bounty of their Heavenly Father.

SHOGHI EFFENDI

29

Freedom from racial prejudice, in any of its forms, should, at such a time as this when an increasingly large section of the human race is falling a victim to its devastating ferocity, be adopted as the watchword of the entire body of the American believers, in whichever state they reside, in whatever circles they move, whatever their age, traditions, tastes, and habits. It should be consistently demonstrated in every phase of their activity and life, whether in the Bahá'í community or outside it, in public or in private, formally as well as informally, individually as well as in their official capacity as organized groups, committees and Assemblies.

30

"God," 'Abdu'l-Bahá Himself declares, "maketh no distinction between the white and the black. If the hearts are pure both are acceptable unto Him. God is no respecter of persons on account of either color or race. All colors are acceptable unto Him, be they white, black, or yellow. Inasmuch as all were created in the image of God, we must bring ourselves to realize that all embody divine possibilities." "In the estimation of God," He states, "all men are equal. There is no distinction or preference for any soul, in the realm of His justice and equity." "God did not make these divisions," He affirms; "these divisions have had their origin in man himself. Therefore, as they are against the plan and purpose of God they are false and imaginary."

31

"No radiance," He [Bahá'u'lláh] declares, "can compare with that of justice. The organization of the world and the tranquility of mankind depend upon it." "O people of God!" He exclaims, "That which traineth the world is Justice, for it is upheld by two pillars, reward and punishment. These two pillars are the sources of life to the world." "Justice and equity," is yet another assertion, "are two guardians for the protection of man. They have appeared arrayed in their mighty and sacred names to maintain the world in uprightness and protect the nations." "Bestir yourselves, O people," is His emphatic warning, "in anticipation of the days of Divine justice, for the promised hour is now come. Beware lest ye fail to apprehend its import, and be accounted among the erring." "The day is approaching," He similarly has written, "when the faithful will behold the daystar of justice shining in its full splendor from the dayspring of glory."

32

"God be praised!" 'Abdu'l-Bahá, in His turn, exclaims, "The sun of justice hath risen above the horizon of Bahá'u'lláh. For in His Tablets the foundations of such a justice have been laid as no mind hath, from the beginning of creation, conceived." "The canopy of existence," He further explains, "resteth upon the pole of justice, and not of forgiveness, and the life of mankind dependeth on justice and not on forgiveness."

Small wonder, therefore, that the Author of the Bahá'í Revelation should have chosen to associate the name and title of that House, which is to be the crowning glory of His administrative institutions, not with forgiveness but with justice, to have made justice the only basis and the permanent foundation of His Most Great Peace, and to have proclaimed it in His Hidden Words as "the best beloved of all things" in His sight. It is to the American believers, particularly, that I feel urged to direct this fervent plea to ponder in their hearts the implications of this moral rectitude, and to uphold, with heart and soul and uncompromisingly, both individually and collectively, this sublime standard—a standard of which justice is so essential and potent an element.

33

A rectitude of conduct, an abiding sense of undeviating justice, unobscured by the demoralizing influences which a corruption-ridden political life so strikingly manifests; a chaste, pure, and holy life, unsullied and unclouded by the indecencies, the vices, the false standards, which an inherently deficient moral code tolerates, perpetuates, and fosters; a fraternity freed from that cancerous growth of racial prejudice, which is eating into the vitals of an already debilitated society—these are the ideals which the American believers must, from now on, individually and through concerted action, strive to promote, in both their private and public lives, ideals which are the chief propelling forces that can most effectively accelerate the march of their institutions, plans, and enterprises, that can guard the honor and integrity of their Faith, and subdue any obstacles that may confront it in the future.

34

God's purpose is none other than to usher in, in ways He alone can bring about, and the full significance of which He alone can fathom, the Great, the Golden Age of a long-divided, a long-afflicted humanity. Its present state, indeed even its immediate future, is dark, distressingly dark. Its distant future, however, is radiant, gloriously radiant—so radiant that no eye can visualize it.

35

The oneness of mankind is the fundamental basis upon which the World Order of Bahá'u'lláh is built. Therefore the Bahá'ís must carry into their lives and into their activities the ideals which Bahá'u'lláh has taught of the unity of the human race.

THE UNIVERSAL
HOUSE OF JUSTICE

36

. . . justice, as a faculty of the soul, enables the individual to distinguish truth from falsehood and guides the investigation of reality, so essential if superstitious beliefs and outworn traditions that impede unity are to be eliminated; that, when appropriately brought to bear on social issues, justice is the single most important instrument for the establishment of unity. . . .

37

And just as the viability of every cell and every organ is contingent upon the health of the body as a whole, so should the prosperity of every individual, every family, every people be sought in the well-being of the entire human race.

38

Racial and ethnic prejudices have been subjected to equally summary treatment by historical processes that have little patience left for such pretensions. Here, rejection of the past has been especially decisive. Racism is now tainted by its association with the horrors of the twentieth century to the degree that it has taken on something of the character of a spiritual disease. While surviving as a social attitude in many parts of the world—and as a blight on the lives of a significant segment of humankind—racial prejudice has become so universally condemned in principle that no body of people can any longer safely allow themselves to be identified with it.

39

If we allow prejudice of any kind to manifest itself in us, we shall be guilty before God of causing a setback to the progress and real growth of the Faith of Bahá'u'lláh. It is incumbent upon every believer to endeavor with a fierce determination to eliminate this defect from his thoughts and acts.

40

Wherever they reside, Bahá'ís endeavour to uphold the standard of justice, addressing inequities directed towards themselves or towards others, but only through lawful means available to them, eschewing all forms of violent protest. Moreover, in no way does the love they hold in their hearts for humanity run counter to the sense of duty they feel to expend their energies in service to their respective countries.

41

Social justice will be attained only when every member of society enjoys a relative degree of material prosperity and gives due regard to the acquisition of spiritual qualities. The solution, then, to prevailing economic difficulties is to be sought as much in the application of spiritual principles as in the implementation of scientific methods and approaches. The family unit offers an ideal setting within which can be shaped those moral attributes that contribute to an appropriate view of material wealth and its utilization.

42

At the very core of the aims of the Faith are the establishment of justice and unity in the world, the removal of prejudice and enmity from among all people, the awakening of compassion and understanding in the hearts of all men and women, and the raising of all souls to a new level of spirituality and behavior through the vitalizing influence of divine Revelation.

43

Bahá'ís perceive humanity as a single body. All are inseparably bound to one another. A social order structured to meet the needs of one group at the expense of another results in injustice and oppression. Instead, the best interest of each component part is achieved by considering its needs in the context of the well-being of the whole.

44

Too often political goals, even when pursued in the name of justice, are a chimera, for the fundamental partisanship in contemporary political life means policies are often implemented without building consensus and consequently seeds of discontent and continuing political struggle are sown. Conflict and contention ultimately yield more conflict and contention. Eliminating social problems, rather than merely ameliorating them to an extent, requires unity of thought as well as action, an open heart as well as an open hand—conditions which Bahá'u'lláh's Revelation is intended to bring about.

45

One of the current features of the process of the disintegration of the old world order manifest in the United States is the increasing polarization and fragmentation that has come to characterize so much of political and social life. There has been a hardening of viewpoints, increased incivility, an unwillingness to compromise or even entertain differing perspectives, and a tendency to automatically take sides and fight. Science and religion, two great lights that should guide human progress, are often compromised or swept aside. Matters of moral principle and questions of justice are reduced to intractable liberal or conservative viewpoints, and the country is increasingly divided along divergent lines. In this context, the friends have to hold steadfastly to the Bahá'í teachings and consultative methods and not allow their pursuit of noble aims and high aspirations to draw them into one side or the other of fruitless debates and contentious processes.

46

As Bahá'u'lláh stated: "Say: no man can attain his true station except through his justice. No power can exist except through unity. No welfare and no well-being can be attained except through consultation." In this light, justice is indeed essential to resist the vain imaginings and idle fancies of social and political machinations, to see reality with one's own eyes, and to identify the requirements for an equitable social order. But then unity is essential—forged through consultative processes, including action and reflection—to achieve the power required for positive social change.

47

The organized endeavors of the Bahá'í community in these areas are reinforced by the diverse initiatives of individual believers working in various fields—as volunteers, professionals, and experts—to contribute to social change. The distinctive nature of their approach is to avoid conflict and the contest for power while striving to unite people in the search for underlying moral and spiritual principles and for practical measures that can lead to the just resolution of the problems afflicting society.

Courage

‘ABDU’L-BAHÁ

1

Do not despair! Work steadily. Sincerity and love will conquer hate. How many seemingly impossible events are coming to pass in these days! Set your faces steadily towards the Light of the World. Show love to all; "Love is the breath of the Holy Spirit in the heart of Man."

2

Consort together in brotherly love, be ready to lay down your lives one for the other, and not only for those who are dear to you, but for all humanity. Look upon the whole human race as members of one family, all children of God; and, in so doing, you will see no difference between them.

3

The great unselfish love for humanity is bounded by none of these imperfect, semi-selfish bonds; this is the one perfect love, possible to all mankind, and can only be achieved by the power of the Divine Spirit. No worldly power can accomplish the universal love.

Let all be united in this Divine power of love! Let all strive to grow in the light of the Sun of Truth, and reflecting this luminous love on all men, may their hearts become so united that they may dwell evermore in the radiance of the limitless love.

4

They consist in justice and equity, truthfulness and benevolence, inner courage and innate humanity, safeguarding the rights of others and preserving the sanctity of covenants and agreements. They consist in rectitude of conduct under all circumstances, love of truth under all conditions, self-abnegation for the good of all people, kindness and compassion for all nations, obedience to the teachings of God, service to the heavenly Kingdom, guidance for all mankind, and education for all races and nations. This is the felicity of the human world! This is the exaltation of man in the contingent realm! This is eternal life and heavenly honor!

SHOGHI EFFENDI

5

Let not, however, the invincible army of Bahá'u'lláh, who in the West, and at one of its potential storm centers is to fight, in His name and for His sake, one of its fiercest and most glorious battles, be afraid of any criticism that might be directed against it. Let it not be deterred by any condemnation with which the tongue of the slanderer may seek to debase its motives. Let it not recoil before the threatening advance of the forces of fanaticism, of orthodoxy, of corruption, and of prejudice that may be leagued against it.

6

We stand on the threshold of an age whose convulsions proclaim alike the death-pangs of the old order and the birth-pangs of the new. Through the generating influence of the Faith announced by Bahá'u'lláh this New World Order may be said to have been conceived. We can, at the present moment, experience its stirrings in the womb of a travailing age—an age waiting for the appointed hour at which it can cast its burden and yield its fairest fruit.

7

As to racial prejudice, the corrosion of which, for well-nigh a century, has bitten into the fiber, and attacked the whole social structure of American society, it should be regarded as constituting the most vital and challenging issue confronting the Bahá'í community at the present stage of its evolution. The ceaseless exertions which this issue of paramount importance calls for, the sacrifices it must impose, the care and vigilance it demands, the moral courage and fortitude it requires, the tact and sympathy it necessitates, invest this problem, which the American believers are still far from having satisfactorily resolved, with an urgency and importance that cannot be overestimated.

8

Delicate and strenuous though the task may be, however arduous and prolonged the effort required, whatsoever the nature of the perils and pitfalls that beset the path of whoever arises to revive the fortunes of a Faith struggling against the rising forces of materialism, nationalism, secularism, racialism, ecclesiasticism, the all-conquering potency of the grace of God, vouchsafed through the Revelation of Bahá'u'lláh, will, undoubtedly, mysteriously and surprisingly, enable whosoever arises to champion His Cause to win complete and total victory.

9

Once its members have fully recognized the claim of its Author, and, by identifying themselves with its Administrative Order, accepted unreservedly the principles and laws embodied in its teachings, every differentiation of class, creed, or color must automatically be obliterated, and never be allowed, under any pretext, and however great the pressure of events or of public opinion, to reassert itself.

10

At such a time as this the believers must take a very firm and strong stand on the racial issue so that there may be no misunderstanding on anyone's part as to just how the Bahá'ís view this all-important subject. . . . The Guardian is praying that this serious problem may find solution in the hearts of the people because its ultimate solution rests with the individual who has become imbued with the ideal of unity and in that field there is no place for segregation.

11

The believers must realize that the forces of prejudice are, along with so many other evil practices, growing at present stronger in the darkness surrounding humanity. The Bahá'ís must exercise not only tact and judgment, but courage and confidence in the aid of Bahá'u'lláh, which He will vouchsafe to those who attempt to live up to His teachings, in their whole approach to this racial question. Too much hesitance, too great timidity in the face of public opinion, can be just as bad as too much disregard of the actual situation and the problems it involves.

12

It is difficult for the friends to always remember that in matter[s] where race enters, a hundred times more consideration and wisdom in handling situations is necessary than when an issue is not complicated by this factor.

13

'Abdu'l-Bahá Himself set the perfect example to the American believers in this matter—as in every other. He was tactful, but the essence of courage, and showed no favoritism to the white people as opposed to their dark-skinned compatriots. No matter how sincere and devoted the white believers in the South may be, there is no reason why they should be the ones to decide when and how the Negro Southerner shall hear of the Cause of God; both must be taught by whoever rises to spread the Message in those parts.

14

The racial problem, whether in America or elsewhere should, indeed, be tackled with the utmost tact and moderation, but also with conscious, firm and absolute loyalty to the spirit as well as to the actual word of the Bahá'í teaching of the Oneness of Mankind.

THE UNIVERSAL
HOUSE OF JUSTICE

15

Whatever suffering and turmoil the years immediately ahead may hold, however dark the immediate circumstances, the Bahá'í community believes that humanity can confront this supreme trial with confidence in its ultimate outcome. Far from signalizing the end of civilization, the convulsive changes towards which humanity is being ever more rapidly impelled will serve to release the "potentialities inherent in the station of man" and reveal "the full measure of his destiny on earth, the innate excellence of his reality."

16

The principle of the oneness of humankind implies, then, an organic change in the very structure of society.

17

In an environment of love and trust born of common belief, practice, and mission, individuals of different races will have the intimate connection of heart and mind upon which mutual understanding and change depend. . . .

Action

BAHÁ'U'LLÁH

1

This span of earth is but one homeland and one habitation. It behooveth you to abandon vainglory which causeth alienation and to set your hearts on whatever will ensure harmony. In the estimation of the people of Bahá man's glory lieth in his knowledge, his upright conduct, his praiseworthy character, his wisdom, and not in his nationality or rank.

2

Say: O men! This is a matchless Day. Matchless must, likewise, be the tongue that celebrateth the praise of the Desire of all nations, and matchless the deed that aspireth to be acceptable in His sight. The whole human race hath longed for this Day, that perchance it may fulfill that which well beseemeth its station, and is worthy of its destiny. Blessed is the man whom the affairs of the world have failed to deter from recognizing Him Who is the Lord of all things.

3

The All-Knowing Physician hath His finger on the pulse of mankind. He perceiveth the disease, and prescribeth, in His unerring wisdom, the remedy. Every age hath its own problem, and every soul its particular aspiration. The remedy the world needeth in its present-day afflictions can never be the same as that which a subsequent age may require. Be anxiously concerned with the needs of the age ye live in, and canter your deliberations on its exigencies and requirements.

4

We can well perceive how the whole human race is encompassed with great, with incalculable afflictions. We see it languishing on its bed of sickness, sore-tried and disillusioned. They that are intoxicated by self-conceit have interposed themselves between it and the Divine and infallible Physician. Witness how they have entangled all men, themselves included, in the mesh of their devices. They can neither discover the cause of the disease, nor have they any knowledge of the remedy. They have conceived the straight to be crooked, and have imagined their friend an enemy.

Incline your ears to the sweet melody of this Prisoner. Arise, and lift up your voices, that haply they that are fast asleep may be awakened. Say: O ye who are as dead! The Hand of Divine bounty proffereth unto you the Water of Life. Hasten and drink your fill. Whoso hath been reborn in this Day, shall never die; whoso remaineth dead, shall never live.

'ABDU'L-BAHÁ

5

It is certain that the greatest of instrumentalities for achieving the advancement and the glory of man, the supreme agency for the enlightenment and the redemption of the world, is love and fellowship and unity among all the members of the human race. Nothing can be effected in the world, not even conceivably, without unity and agreement, and the perfect means for engendering fellowship and union is true religion. "Hadst Thou spent all the riches of the earth, Thou couldst not have united their hearts; but God hath united them . . . "*

---

* Qur'an 8:64.

6

O ye beloved of God! Know ye, verily, that the happiness of mankind lieth in the unity and the harmony of the human race, and that spiritual and material developments are conditioned upon love and amity among all men.

7

Raise ye a clamor like unto a roaring sea; like a prodigal cloud, rain down the grace of heaven. Lift up your voices and sing out the songs of the Abhá Realm. Quench ye the fires of war, lift high the banners of peace, work for the oneness of humankind and remember that religion is the channel of love unto all peoples.

8

Strive with heart and soul in order to bring about union and harmony among the white and the black and prove thereby the unity of the Bahá'í world wherein distinction of color findeth no place, but where hearts only are considered. Praise be to God, the hearts of the friends are united and linked together, whether they be from the east or the west, from north or from south, whether they be German, French, Japanese, American, and whether they pertain to the white, the black, the red, the yellow or the brown race. Variations of color, of land and of race are of no importance in the Bahá'í Faith; on the contrary, Bahá'í unity overcometh them all and doeth away with all these fancies and imaginations.

9

Wherefore must the loved ones of God associate in affectionate fellowship with stranger and friend alike, showing forth to all the utmost lovingkindness, disregarding the degree of their capacity, never asking whether they deserve to be loved. In every instance let the friends be considerate and infinitely kind. Let them never be defeated by the malice of the people, by their aggression and their hate, no matter how intense. If others hurl their darts against you, offer them milk and honey in return; if they poison your lives, sweeten their souls; if they injure you, teach them how to be comforted; if they inflict a wound upon you, be a balm to their sores; if they sting you, hold to their lips a refreshing cup.

10

Wherefore, O my loving friends! Consort with all the peoples, kindreds and religions of the world with the utmost truthfulness, uprightness, faithfulness, kindliness, good-will and friendliness, that all the world of being may be filled with the holy ecstasy of the grace of Bahá, that ignorance, enmity, hate and rancor may vanish from the world and the darkness of estrangement amidst the peoples and kindreds of the world may give way to the Light of Unity.

11

For the accomplishment of unity between the colored and whites will be an assurance of the world's peace. Then racial prejudice, national prejudice, limited patriotism and religious bias will pass away and remain no longer.

12

Briefly, we must strive with heart and soul in order that this darkness of the contingent world may be dispelled, that the lights of the Kingdom shall shine upon all the horizons, the world of humanity become illumined, the image of God become apparent in human mirrors, the law of God be well established and that all regions of the world shall enjoy peace, comfort and composure beneath the equitable protection of God.

13

Consider how the greatest men in the world—whether among prophets or philosophers—all have forfeited their own comfort, have sacrificed their own pleasure for the well-being of humanity. They have sacrificed their own lives for the body politic. They have sacrificed their own wealth for that of the general welfare. They have forfeited their own honor for the honor of mankind. Therefore, it becomes evident that this is the highest attainment for the world of humanity.

SHOGHI EFFENDI

14

Let there be no mistake. The principle of the Oneness of Mankind—the pivot round which all the teachings of Bahá'u'lláh revolve—is no mere outburst of ignorant emotionalism or an expression of vague and pious hope. Its appeal is not to be merely identified with a reawakening of the spirit of brotherhood and good-will among men, nor does it aim solely at the fostering of harmonious cooperation among individual peoples and nations. Its implications are deeper, its claims greater than any which the Prophets of old were allowed to advance. Its message is applicable not only to the individual, but concerns itself primarily with the nature of those essential relationships that must bind all the states and nations as members of one human family.

15

Let them call to mind, fearlessly and determinedly, the example and conduct of 'Abdu'l-Bahá while in their midst. Let them remember His courage, His genuine love, His informal and indiscriminating fellowship, His contempt for and impatience of criticism, tempered by His tact and wisdom. Let them revive and perpetuate the memory of those unforgettable and historic episodes and occasions on which He so strikingly demonstrated His keen sense of justice, His spontaneous sympathy for the downtrodden, His ever-abiding sense of the oneness of the human race, His overflowing love for its members, and His displeasure with those who dared to flout His wishes, to deride His methods, to challenge His principles, or to nullify His acts.

16

The whole of mankind is groaning, is dying to be led to unity, and to terminate its age-long martyrdom. And yet it stubbornly refuses to embrace the light and acknowledge the sovereign authority of the one Power that can extricate it from its entanglements, and avert the woeful calamity that threatens to engulf it.

17

All must participate, however humble their origin, however limited their experience, however restricted their means, however deficient their education, however pressing their cares and preoccupations, however unfavorable the environment in which they live.

18

How great, therefore, how staggering the responsibility that must weigh upon the present generation of the American believers, at this early stage in their spiritual and administrative evolution, to weed out, by every means in their power, those faults, habits, and tendencies which they have inherited from their own nation, and to cultivate, patiently and prayerfully, those distinctive qualities and characteristics that are so indispensable to their effective participation in the great redemptive work of their Faith.

19

The gross materialism that engulfs the entire nation at the present hour; the attachment to worldly things that enshrouds the souls of men; the fears and anxieties that distract their minds; the pleasure and dissipations that fill their time, the prejudices and animosities that darken their outlook, the apathy and lethargy that paralyze their spiritual faculties—these are among the formidable obstacles that stand in the path of every would-be warrior in the service of Bahá'u'lláh, obstacles which he must battle against and surmount in his crusade for the redemption of his own countrymen.

20

Let every believer, desirous to witness the swift and healthy progress of the Cause of God, realize the twofold nature of his task. Let him first turn his eyes inwardly and search his own heart and satisfy himself that in his relations with his fellow-believers, irrespective of color and class, he is proving himself increasingly loyal to the spirit of his beloved Faith. Assured and content that he is exerting his utmost in a conscious effort to approach nearer every day the lofty station to which his gracious Master summons him, let him turn to his second task, and, with befitting confidence and vigor, assail the devastating power of those forces which in his own heart he has already succeeded in subduing. Fully alive to the unfailing efficacy of the power of Bahá'u'lláh, and armed with the essential weapons of wise restraint and inflexible resolve, let him wage a constant fight against the inherited tendencies, the corruptive instincts, the fluctuating fashions, the false pretences of the society in which he lives and moves.

21

If we relax in our purpose, if we falter in our faith, if we neglect the varied opportunities given us from time to time by an all-wise and gracious Master, we are not merely failing in what is our most vital and conspicuous obligation, but are thereby insensibly retarding the flow of those quickening energies which can alone insure the vigorous and speedy development of God's struggling Faith.

22

No more laudable and meritorious service can be rendered the Cause of God, at the present hour, than a successful effort to enhance the diversity of the members of the American Bahá'í community by swelling the ranks of the Faith through the enrollment of the members of these races [the Negro, the Indian, the Eskimo, and Jewish]. A blending of these highly differentiated elements of the human race, harmoniously interwoven into the fabric of an all-embracing Bahá'í fraternity, and assimilated through the dynamic processes of a divinely appointed Administrative Order, and contributing each its share to the enrichment and glory of Bahá'í community life, is surely an achievement the contemplation of which must warm and thrill every Bahá'í heart.

23

If any discrimination is at all to be tolerated, it should be a discrimination not against, but rather in favor of the minority, be it racial or otherwise. Unlike the nations and peoples of the earth, be they of the East or of the West, democratic or authoritarian, communist or capitalist, whether belonging to the Old World or the New, who either ignore, trample upon, or extirpate, the racial, religious, or political minorities within the sphere of their jurisdiction, every organized community enlisted under the banner of Bahá'u'lláh should feel it to be its first and inescapable obligation to nurture, encourage, and safeguard every minority belonging to any faith, race, class, or nation within it.

24

Now, as to the methods which the friends should adopt for the application of this principle [of the oneness of mankind]; the Guardian has invariably urged the believers to act with the utmost wisdom, tact and moderation. It is not only fruitless, but actually harmful to the best interests of the Cause to publicly and violently attack the racial corruptions and traditions prevalent among such a large section of the American people. The friends should first start by applying the principle of the oneness of races within their own community, and thus set before the world outside a noble and inspiring example. Every trace of racial prejudice should be banished by the friends in their community life, and also in their private life, so much so that they should come to gradually forget the very existence of the racial problem as such. Such an attitude is bound to strongly impress every outsider and draw his attention to the Cause, and convince him of the sublimity and practicability of its Teachings.

25

He was particularly happy to see that some of the Indian believers were present at the Convention. He attaches the greatest importance to teaching the original inhabitants of the Americas the Faith. 'Abdu'l-Bahá Himself has stated how great are their potentialities, and it is their right, and the duty of the non-Indian Bahá'ís, to see that they receive the Message of God for this Day. One of the most worthy objectives of your Assembly must be the establishment of all-Indian Spiritual Assemblies. Other minorities should likewise be especially sought out and taught.

26

The friends must, at all times, bear in mind that they are, in a way, like soldiers under attack. The world is at present in an exceedingly dark condition spiritually; hatred and prejudice, of every sort, are literally tearing it to pieces. We, on the other hand, are the custodians of the opposite forces, the forces of love, of unity, of peace and integration, and we must constantly be on our guard, whether as individuals or as an Assembly or Community, lest through us these destructive, negative forces enter into our midst. In other words we must beware lest the darkness of society become reflected in our acts and attitudes, perhaps all unconsciously. Love for each other, the deep sense that we are a new organism, the dawn-breakers for a New World Order, must constantly animate our Bahá'í lives, and we must pray to be protected from the contamination of society which is so diseased with prejudice.

27

By all means persevere and associate in a friendly spirit with other groups of young people, particularly of a different race or minority nationality, for such association will demonstrate your complete conviction of the oneness of mankind and attract others to the Faith, both young and old alike.

A spirit of prejudice-free, loving comradeship with others is what will open the eyes of people more than any amount of words. Combined with such deeds you can teach the Faith easily.

28

In America, where racial prejudice is still so widely prevalent, it is the responsibility of the believers to combat and uproot it with all their force, first by endeavouring to introduce into the Cause as many . . . minority groups as they can approach and teach, and second by stimulating close fellowship and intercourse between them and the rest of the Community.

THE UNIVERSAL
HOUSE OF JUSTICE

29

The question that occupies the worldwide Bahá'í community, then, is how it can best contribute to the civilization-building process as its resources increase. It sees two dimensions to its contribution. The first is related to its own growth and development, and the second to its involvement in society at large.

30

When Bahá'u'lláh proclaimed His Message to the world in the nineteenth century He made it abundantly clear that the first step essential for the peace and progress of mankind was its unification. As He says, "The well-being of mankind, its peace and security are unattainable unless and until its unity is firmly established." To this day, however, you will find most people take the opposite point of view: they look upon unity as an ultimate almost unattainable goal and concentrate first on remedying all the other ills of mankind. If they did but know it, these other ills are but various symptoms and side effects of the basic disease—disunity.

31

The solution to these problems lies not so much in the formulation of workable theories; it is related to the overall spiritual transformation which is to take place through the gradual influence of the Bahá'í teachings on the lives of people throughout the world—a transformation which will itself be the matrix for the solution so anxiously sought. In the meantime, governments, through hard experience, will, no doubt, take steps which are in harmony with the progressive spirit of the times.

32

Unity, in its Bahá'í expression, contains the essential concept of diversity, distinguishing it from uniformity. It is through love for all people, and by subordinating lesser loyalties to the best interests of humankind, that the unity of the world can be realized and the infinite expressions of human diversity find their highest fulfilment.

33

However long and arduous the road that must be travelled, we are supremely confident in your fortitude and your determination to see the journey through. You draw from stores of hope, faith, and magnanimity, putting the needs of others before your own, enabling those who are deprived to be spiritually nourished, those who increasingly thirst for answers to be satisfied, and those who long to work for the betterment of the world to be offered the means. From the devoted followers of the Blessed Perfection, how could we expect less?

34

Yet, however promising the rise in collective consciousness may be, it should be seen as only the first step of a process that will take decades—nay, centuries—to unfold. For the principle of the oneness of humankind, as proclaimed by Bahá'u'lláh, asks not merely for cooperation among people and nations. It calls for a complete reconceptualization of the relationships that sustain society.

35

Ahead of you lie times of trial and promise, of hardship and progress, of anguish and joy. Under all conditions, the Master is your solace and support. For those who aspire to lasting change, His example guides the way— tactful and wise in His approach, penetrating in utterance, indiscriminating in fellowship, unfailing in sympathy for the downtrodden, courageous in conduct, persevering in action, imperturbable in the face of tests, unwavering in His keen sense of justice. And to all who arise to emulate Him, He offers this unfailing assurance: "that which is confirmed is the oneness of the world of humanity. Every soul who serveth this oneness will undoubtedly be assisted and confirmed."

36

The Universal House of Justice sympathizes with your view that the situation in America has not changed as hoped, but as the beloved Guardian has told us in the *Advent of Divine Justice*, no profound and lasting change will come about unless certain spiritual prerequisites are met. These prerequisites have yet to be achieved by the broad public, and Bahá'ís themselves have often been slow to put them into practice.

37

The key to resolving these social ills rests in the hands of a youthful generation convinced of the nobility of human beings; eagerly seeking a deeper understanding of the true purpose of existence; able to distinguish between divine religion and mere superstition; clear in the view of science and religion as two independent yet complementary systems of knowledge that propel human progress; conscious of and drawn to the beauty and power of unity in diversity; secure in the knowledge that real glory is to be found in service to one's country and to the peoples of the world; and mindful that the acquisition of wealth is praiseworthy only insofar as it is attained through just means and expended for benevolent purposes, for the promotion of knowledge and toward the common good. Thus must our precious youth prepare themselves to shoulder the tremendous responsibilities that await them. And thus will they prove immune to the atmosphere of greed that surrounds them and press forward unwavering in the pursuit of their exalted goals.

38

Humanity's crying need will not be met by a struggle among competing ambitions or by protest against one or another of the countless wrongs afflicting a desperate age. It calls, rather, for a fundamental change of consciousness, for a wholehearted embrace of Bahá'u'lláh's teaching that the time has come when each human being on earth must learn to accept responsibility for the welfare of the entire human family.

39

The overall direction of the process of learning that the Bahá'í community is pursuing is guided by a series of global plans, the provisions of which are established by the Universal House of Justice. Capacity building is the watchword of these plans: they aim at enabling the protagonists of collective effort to strengthen the spiritual foundations of villages and neighbourhoods, to address certain of their social and economic needs, and to contribute to the discourses prevalent in society, all while maintaining the necessary coherence in methods and approaches.

40

Bahá'ís, of course, strive to align them-selves, individually and collectively, with forces associated with the process of integra-tion, which, they are confident, will continue to gain in strength, no matter how bleak the immediate horizons. Human affairs will be utterly reorganized, and an era of universal peace inaugurated.

41

The real secret of universal participation lies in the Master's oft expressed wish that the friends should love each other, constantly encourage each other, work together, be as one soul in one body, and in so doing become a true, organic, healthy body animated and illumined by the spirit. In such a body all will receive spiritual health and vitality from the organism itself, and the most perfect flowers and fruits will be brought forth.

42

What should be stated plainly here is that Bahá'ís do not believe the transformation thus envisioned will come about exclusively through their own efforts. Nor are they trying to create a movement that would seek to impose on society their vision of the future. Every nation and every group—indeed, every individual—will, to a greater or lesser degree, contribute to the emergence of the world civilization towards which humanity is irresistibly moving. Unity will progressively be achieved, as foreshadowed by 'Abdu'l-Bahá, in different realms of social existence, for instance, "unity in the political realm," "unity of thought in world undertakings," "unity of races" and the "unity of nations." As these come to be realized, the structures of a politically united world, which respects the full diversity of culture and provides channels for the expression of dignity and honour, will gradually take shape.

43

Efforts to reach the minorities should be increased and broadened to include all minority groups such as the Indians, Spanish-speaking people, Japanese and Chinese. Indeed, every stratum of American society must be reached and can be reached with the healing Message, if the believers will but arise and go forth with the spirit which is conquering the citadels of the southern states. Such a program, coupled as it must be with continuous consolidation, can be effectively carried out by universal participation on the part of every lover of Bahá'u'lláh.

44

Yet change is not confined merely to the Bahá'ís and those who are involved in the core activities called for by the Plan, who might reasonably be expected to adopt new ways of thinking over time. The very spirit of the place is affected. A devotional attitude takes shape within a broad sweep of the population. Expressions of the equality of men and women become more pronounced. The education of children, both boys and girls, commands greater attention. The character of relationships within families—moulded by assumptions centuries old—alters perceptibly. A sense of duty towards one's immediate community and physical environment becomes prevalent. Even the scourge of prejudice, which casts its baleful shadow on every society, begins to yield to the compelling force of unity. In short, the community-building work in which the friends are engaged influences aspects of culture.

45

In recent years it has become evident that in communities where there has been a strong emphasis on the capacity-building features of the Five Year Plan, the ability of the friends to engage in social action has increased substantially. Accordingly, you would do well to encourage the friends to persevere in their efforts to strengthen the training institute and the activities of the Plan, for therein lies the key to multiplying your human resources and creating a vibrant, united, and loving community. As they progress along this path, they will become increasingly capable of contributing in tangible ways to the practical resolution of the problems that confront populations at the grassroots in cities and towns, neighbourhoods and villages.

46

What is needed is concerted, persistent, sacrificial action, cycle after cycle, in cluster after cluster, by an ever-swelling number of consecrated individuals.

In the next year you will observe the centenary of the visit of 'Abdu'l-Bahá to your shores and will recall His tireless and heroic exertions to quicken the peoples of America—in particular His fearless assault on racial barriers. Follow in His noble path, so that by the end of this new Plan and the one to follow, you will have an abundant harvest of victories to offer in His name by the centenary of His passing in 2021.

47

Unfortunately, sometimes when approaching such important and deeply-felt matters, the friends can create dichotomies where none exist. Thus, for example, it is contended that one must choose between either non-involvement in politics or social action; either teaching the Faith or involvement with society; either the institute process and the community-building activities it fosters or a program for race unity; and so on. Such apparent conflicts can be greatly dissipated by keeping in mind Shoghi Effendi's advice, conveyed in a letter written on his behalf, to conceive of the teachings as one great whole with many facets. "Truth may, in covering different subjects, appear to be contradictory," the same letter indicated, "and yet it is all one if you carry the thought through to the end." A careful reading of the Bahá'í writings and the guidance of the House of Justice can clarify how two matters that appear to be in tension with one another are coherent once the concepts and principles that connect them are understood. Particular circumstances in a locality, timeliness, and the periodic need for focus also have a bearing on such issues.

48

In a recent letter written on its behalf, the House of Justice explained to your National Assembly that the scope of the Five Year Plan offers ample opportunities for believers to address the social concerns of their communities and society as a whole. The Plan's activities for sustained growth and community building lie at the heart of a broad scheme for social transformation. The friends are called to three simultaneous, overlapping, and coherent areas of action: community-building efforts in clusters; projects and activities for social action; and involvement in the discourses of society, whether in neighborhoods or in personal or professional associations.

49

The principles of non-involvement in politics and obedience to government, far from being obstacles to social change, are aspects of an approach set forth in the Bahá'í writings to implement effective remedies for and address the root causes of the ills afflicting society. This approach includes active involvement in the life of society as well as the possibility of influencing and contributing to the social policies of government by all lawful means. Indeed, service to others and to society is a hallmark of the Bahá'í life.

50

. . . effective social action will result, then, as capacity at the grassroots of the community increases and collective consciousness is raised.

51

As the learning process that has proven to be so effective in the expansion and consolidation work worldwide is increasingly employed in all endeavors, the capacity of individuals, communities, and institutions to apply Bahá'u'lláh's healing remedy to achieve profound and lasting change will become ever more pronounced, assisting the nation along the path of its destiny.

52

There can be no question then that Bahá'ís are committed to efforts toward social transformation. "Much as the friends must guard against in any way ever seeming to identify themselves or the Cause with any political party," Shoghi Effendi, through his secretary, cautioned, "they must also guard against the other extreme of never taking part, with other progressive groups, in conferences or committees designed to promote some activity in entire accord with our teachings—such as, for instance, better race relations." This involvement in activities for social reform and well-being can in certain circumstances even extend to taking part in demonstrations. A letter written on the Guardian's behalf indicated that he did not see any objection to Bahá'í students taking part as Bahá'ís in a protest concerning racial prejudice on campus, since "there was nothing political about it" and "he does not see how they could remain indifferent when fellow-students were voicing our own Bahá'í attitude on such a vital issue and one we feel so strongly about." Thus, individual Bahá'ís are free to participate in those efforts and activities, such as peaceful rallies, that uphold constructive aims in consonance with the Bahá'í teachings, for example, the advancement of women, the promotion of social justice, the protection of the environment, the elimination of all forms of discrimination, and the safeguarding of human rights.

53

In their reflections on how to contribute to the betterment of the world, Bahá'ís will undoubtedly recognize that demonstrations are not the only, or even the most effective, means available to them. Rather, they can learn and grow in capacity over time to help their fellow citizens to frame concerns in a way that rises above fissures, to share views in a manner that transcends divisive approaches, and to create and participate in spaces to work together in the quest to enact solutions to the problems that bedevil their nation.

54

But for those who have turned towards Him, the vision of human purpose given by the Divine Word illumines the way forward for all peoples. The legacy of pain passed down from the global history of man's cruelty to man so burdens and confuses peoples of various climes that there can be no more immediate necessity than to spread knowledge of that Word far and wide. Has it not conveyed the vital truth that "the Ancient Beauty hath consented to be bound with chains that mankind may be released from its bondage, and hath accepted to be made a prisoner within this most mighty Stronghold that the whole world may attain unto true liberty?" Surely, for any believer knowing this, the foremost act, the most important duty, is to present the Bahá'í message to all who will receive it now.

55

The problems related to class prejudice which you have experienced and observed are noted, and the suggestions you offer for working toward their remedy are truly appreciated. As you know, the Bahá'ís are distinguished not by their perfection or their immunity from the negative influences of the wider society in which they live, but by their acceptance of Bahá'u'lláh's vision and willingness to work toward it. Each of us must strike a balance between realistically facing our community's shortcomings, and focusing on Bahá'u'lláh's Teachings rather than our fellow believers as our standard of faith. This comment is not intended to belittle your concerns, but rather to place them in perspective so that you may not become discouraged as you strive toward the ideal.

NOTES

Justice

BAHÁ'U'LLÁH

1. *Tablets of Bahá'u'lláh,* pp. 164–65.
2. *Bahá'í Prayers,* p. 173.
3. *Epistle to the Son of the Wolf,* pp. 28–29.
4. Ibid., p. 32.
5. *Tablets of Bahá'u'lláh,* p. 66.
6. *Epistle to the Son of the Wolf,* pp. 12–13.
7. The Hidden Words, Arabic, no. 2.
8. *Tablets of Bahá'u'lláh,* p. 36.
9. Ibid., p. 260.
10. *Gleanings from the Writings of Bahá'u'lláh,* no. 63.2.
11. Ibid., no. 118.1.
12. Ibid., no. 132.4.
13. From a Tablet translated from the Arabic, in *The Compilation of Compilations,* vol. I, no. 167.

14. *Gleanings from the Writings of Bahá'u'lláh,* no. 107.1.

'ABDU'L-BAHÁ

15. *The Secret of Divine Civilization,* ¶71.
16. *Selections from the Writings of 'Abdu'l-Bahá,* no. 202.3.
17. *The Secret of Divine Civilization,* ¶5.
18. *Huqúqu'lláh: The Right of God,* no. 61.
19. *Paris Talks,* no. 40.17–18.
20. *The Promulgation of Universal Peace,* pp. 441–42.
21. *Paris Talks,* no. 49.17.
22. Ibid., no. 49.15.
23. *The Promulgation of Universal Peace,* p. 182.
24. Ibid., p. 57.
25. Ibid., p. 252.
26. Ibid., pp. 334–35.
27. Ibid., p. 252.
28. *Paris Talks,* no. 45.11–12.

SHOGHI EFFENDI

29. *The Advent of Divine Justice,* ¶54.
30. Ibid., ¶56.
31. Ibid., ¶42.
32. Ibid., ¶43–44.
33. Ibid., ¶38.
34. *The Promised Day is Come,* ¶286.
35. Letter written on behalf of Shoghi Effendi, dated 27 October 1957, to an individual believer, in *Bahá'í News,* vol. 4, no. 324.

THE UNIVERSAL HOUSE OF JUSTICE

36. From a letter of the Universal House of Justice, dated 2 March 2013, to the Bahá'ís of Iran.

37. Ibid.

38. *To the World's Religious Leaders,* p. 1.

39. *Messages 1963–1986,* no. 117.2–5.

40. From a letter of the Universal House of Justice, dated 2 March 2013, to the Bahá'ís of Iran.

41. From of a letter of the Universal House of Justice, dated 2 April 2010, to the Believers in the Cradle of the Faith.

42. From a letter written on behalf of the Universal House of Justice, dated 2 July 1996, to an individual believer.

43. From a letter written on behalf of the Universal House of Justice, dated 23 December 2008, written to an individual believer.

44. From a letter written on behalf of the Universal House of Justice, dated 27 April, 2017, to an individual believer.

45. Ibid.

46. Ibid.

47. From a letter written on behalf of the Universal House of Justice, dated 23 December 2008, written to an individual believer.

Courage

'ABDU'L-BAHÁ

1. *Paris Talks,* no. 6.12.

2. Ibid., no. 53.11.

3. Ibid., no. 9.3–15.

4. *Some Answered Questions,* no. 15.7.

SHOGHI EFFENDI

5. *The Advent of Divine Justice,* ¶59–61.

6. *The World Order of Bahá'u'lláh,* pp. 168–69.

7. *The Advent of Divine Justice,* ¶51–52.

8. *Citadel of Faith,* p. 148.

9. *The Advent of Divine Justice,* ¶53.

10. From a letter written on behalf of Shoghi Effendi, dated 27 October 1957, to an individual believer, in *Bahá'í News,* vol. 4, no. 324.

11. From a letter written on behalf of Shoghi Effendi, dated 23 December 1941, to an individual believer, in *Lights of Guidance,* no. 1813.

12. From a letter written on behalf of Shoghi Effendi, dated 25 March, 1949, to an individual believer.

13. From a letter written on behalf of Shoghi Effendi, dated 5 July 1942, addressed to an individual believer.

14. From a letter written on behalf of Shoghi Effendi, dated 26 January 1937, to an individual believer, attached to a letter written on behalf of the Universal House of Justice, dated 4 February 1985, to the National Spiritual Assembly of the United States.

THE UNIVERSAL HOUSE OF JUSTICE

15. From a letter of the Universal House of Justice, dated October 1985, addressed to the Peoples of the World.
16. From a letter of the Universal House of Justice, dated 2 March 2013, to the Bahá'ís of Iran.
17. From a letter written on behalf of the Universal House of Justice, dated 10 April 2011, to an individual believer.

Action

BAHÁ'U'LLÁH

1. *Tablets of Bahá'u'lláh*, p. 67.
2. *Gleanings from the Writings of Bahá'u'lláh*, no. 16.1.
3. Ibid., no. 106.1.
4. *The Tabernacle of Unity*, no. 1.6–7.

'ABDU'L-BAHÁ

5. *The Secret of Divine Civilization*, ¶135.
6. *Selections from the Writings of 'Abdu'l-Bahá*, no. 225.10.
7. Ibid., no. 17.4.
8. Ibid., no. 75.1.
9. Ibid., no. 8.8.
10. *Will and Testament of 'Abdu'l-Bahá*, ¶1.24.
11. Quoted in Shoghi Effendi, *The Advent of Divine Justice*, ¶56
12. *The Promulgation of Universal Peace*, p. 405.
13. Ibid., p. 442.

14. *The World Order of Bahá'u'lláh,* p. 42.

15. *The Advent of Divine Justice,* ¶52.

16. *The World Order of Bahá'u'lláh,* p. 201.

17. *The Advent of Divine Justice,* ¶66.

18. Ibid., ¶34.

19. *Citadel of Faith,* p. 148.

20. From a letter, dated 12 April 1927, to the National Spiritual Assembly of the United States and Canada, in *Bahá'í Administration,* pp. 129–30.

21. From a letter, dated 12 April 1927, to the National Spiritual Assembly of the United States and Canada, in Ibid., pp. 129–30.

22. *The Advent of Divine Justice,* ¶81.

23. Ibid., ¶53.

24. From a letter written on behalf of Shoghi Effendi, dated 11 November 1936, to an individual believer.

25. From a letter written on behalf of Shoghi Effendi, in *The Bahá'í World,* vol. 13, p. 104.

26. From a letter written on behalf of Shoghi Effendi, dated 5 February 1947, to the Spiritual Assembly of Atlanta, in *Lights of Guidance,* no. 1347.

27. From a letter written on behalf of Shoghi Effendi, dated 18 June 1945, to the Bahá'ís of Dayton, Ohio, in *The Compilation of Compilations,* vol. II, no. 1958.

28. From a letter written on behalf of Shoghi Effendi, letter dated 30 January 1941, to an individual believer.

THE UNIVERSAL HOUSE OF JUSTICE

29. From a letter of the Universal House of Justice, dated 2 March 2013, to the Bahá'ís of Iran.

30. *Messages 1963 to 1986,* no. 55.3.

31. From a letter of the Universal House of Justice, dated 6 July 1989, in "Economics, Agriculture, and Related Subjects."

32. From a letter of the Universal House of Justice, dated 18 January 2019, to the Bahá'ís of the World.

33. From a letter of the Universal House of Justice, dated Riḍván 2020, to the Bahá'ís of the World.

34. From a letter of the Universal House of Justice, dated 2 March 2013, to the Bahá'ís of Iran.

35. From a letter of the Universal House of Justice, dated 22 July 2020, addressed to the Bahá'ís of the United States.

36. From a letter of the Universal House of Justice, dated 23 May 1990, to an individual believer.

37. From a letter of the Universal House of Justice, dated 2 April 2010, to the Believers in the Cradle of the Faith.

38. From a letter of the Universal House of Justice, dated 24 May 2001, to the Believers Gathered for the Events Marking the Completion of the Projects on Mount Carmel.

39. From a letter of the Universal House of Justice, dated 2 March 2013, to the Bahá'ís of Iran.

40. Ibid.

41. From a letter of the Universal House of Justice, dated September 1964, to the Bahá'ís of the World.

42. From a letter of the Universal House of Justice, dated 2 March 2013, to the Bahá'ís of Iran.

43. From a letter of the Universal House of Justice, dated 14 February 1972, to the National Spiritual Assembly of the United States, in *Messages, 1968–1973*, p. 85.

44. From a letter of the Universal House of Justice, dated Riḍván 2013, to the Bahá'ís of the World.

45. From a letter written on behalf of the Universal House of Justice, dated 1 October 2015, to a National Spiritual Assembly.

46. From a letter written on behalf of the Universal House of Justice, dated 28 August 2011, addressed to the participants of the Black Men's Gathering.

47. From a letter written on behalf of the Universal House of Justice, dated 27 April 2017, to an individual believer.

48. Ibid.

49. Ibid.

50. From a letter written on behalf of the Universal House of Justice, dated 6 September 2006, to an individual believer.

51. From a letter written on behalf of the Universal House of Justice, dated 27 April 2017, to an individual believer.
52. Ibid.
53. Ibid.
54. From a letter written on behalf of the Universal House of Justice, dated 3 June 2007, to an individual believer.
55. From a letter written on behalf of the Universal House of Justice, dated 20 January 1994, to an individual believer.

BIBLIOGRAPHY

Works of Bahá'u'lláh

Epistle to the Son of the Wolf. New ed. Translated by
Shoghi Effendi. 1st ps ed. Wilmette, IL:
Bahá'í Publishing Trust, 1988.

Gleanings from the Writings of Bahá'u'lláh. Translated by Shoghi Effendi. Wilmette, IL:
Bahá'í Publishing, 2005.

The Hidden Words. Translated by Shoghi Effendi.
Wilmette, IL: Bahá'í Publishing, 2002.

*The Tabernacle of Unity: Bahá'u'lláh's Responses to
Mánikchí Ṣáḥib and Other Writings.* Haifa:
Bahá'í World Center, 2006.

Tablets of Bahá'u'lláh revealed after the Kitáb-i-Aqdas.
Compiled by the Research Department of
the Universal House of Justice. Translated
by Habib Taherzadeh et al. Wilmette, IL:
Bahá'í Publishing Trust, 1988.

Works of 'Abdu'l-Bahá

Paris Talks: Addresses Given By 'Abdu'l-Bahá in Paris in 1911. Wilmette, IL: Bahá'í Publishing, 2011.

Promulgation of Universal Peace: Talks Delivered by 'Abdu'l-Bahá during His Visit to the United States and Canada in 1912. Compiled by Howard MacNutt. Wilmette, IL: Bahá'í Publishing, 2012.

The Secret of Divine Civilization. Translated by Marzieh Gail and Ali-Kuli Khan. Wilmette, IL: Bahá'í Publishing, 2007.

Selections from the Writings of 'Abdu'l-Bahá. Compiled by the Research Department of the Universal House of Justice. Translated by a Committee at the Bahá'í World Center and Marzieh Gail. Wilmette, IL: Bahá'í Publishing, 2010.

Some Answered Questions. Newly translated by a Committee at the Bahá'í World Center. Haifa, Israel: Bahá'í World Centre, 2014.

Will and Testament of 'Abdu'l-Bahá. Wilmette, IL: Bahá'í Publishing Trust, 2011.

Works of Shoghi Effendi

Advent of Divine Justice. 1st pocket-size ed. Wilmette, IL: Bahá'í Publishing Trust, 1990.

Bahá'í Administration: Selected Messages 1922–1932. 7th ed. Wilmette, IL: Bahá'í Publishing Trust, 1974.

Citadel of Faith: Messages to America, 1947–1957. Wilmette, IL: Bahá'í Publishing Trust, 1965.

Directives from the Guardian. Wilmette, IL: Bahá'í Publishing Trust, 1973.

The Promised Day Is Come. 1st pocket-size ed. Wilmette, IL: Bahá'í Publishing Trust, 1996.

The World Order of Bahá'u'lláh: Selected Letters. 1st pocket-size ed. Wilmette, IL: Bahá'í Publishing Trust, 1991.

Works of the Universal House of Justice

Messages from the Universal House of Justice, 1963–1986: The Third Epoch of the Formative Age. Compiled by Geoffry Marks. Wilmette, IL: Bahá'í Publishing Trust, 1996.

Messages from the Universal House of Justice, 1986–2001: The Fourth Epoch of the Formative Age. Compiled by Geoffry Marks. Wilmette, IL: Bahá'í Publishing Trust, 2010.

Messages from the Universal House of Justice, 1968–1973. Haifa: Bahá'í World Center, 1973.

The Promise of World Peace: To the Peoples of the World. Wilmette, IL: Bahá'í Publishing Trust, 1985.

To the World's Religious Leaders: A Message from the Universal House of Justice. Wilmette, IL: Bahá'í Publishing Trust, 2002.

Bahá'í Compilations and Other Works

Bahá'í Prayers: A Selection of Prayers Revealed by Bahá'u'lláh, the Báb, and 'Abdu'l-Bahá. New ed. Wilmette, IL: Bahá'í Publishing Trust, 2002.

The Bahá'í World: A Biennial International Record, Vol. 13 (1954–1963). Haifa: Bahá'í World Center, 1970.

The Compilation of Compilations: Prepared by the Universal House of Justice, 1963–1990. 2 vols. Australia: Bahá'í Publications Australia, 1991.

Ḥuqúqu'lláh—The Right of God: A Compilation of Extracts from the Writings of Bahá'u'lláh and 'Abdu'l-Bahá and from Letters Written by and on Behalf of Shoghi Effendi and the Universal House of Justice. Haifa: Bahá'í World Center, 2006.

Lights of Guidance: A Bahá'í Reference File. Compiled by Helen Hornby. New ed. New Dehli, India: Bahá'í Publishing Trust, 1994.